Olympic Greats

OLYMPIC TRACK AND FIELD LEGENDS

MARTIN GITLIN

BLACK
RABBIT
BOOKS

BOLT

Bolt is published by Black Rabbit Books
P.O. Box 3263, Mankato, Minnesota, 56002
www.blackrabbitbooks.com
Copyright © 2021 Black Rabbit Books

Jen Besel, editor; Catherine Cates, designer;
Omay Ayres, photo researcher

Library of Congress Cataloging-in-Publication Data
Names: Gitlin, Marty, author.
Title: Olympic track and field legends / by Martin Gitlin.
Other titles: Track & field legends | Bolt (North Mankato, Minn.)
Description: Mankato, Minnesota : Bolt is published by Black Rabbit Books,
2021 | Series: Bolt. Olympic greats | Includes webography. | Includes
bibliographic references and index. | Audience: Ages 8-12 years |
Audience: Grades 4-6 Identifiers: LCCN 2019027609 (print) | ISBN 9781623102685
(Hardcover) | ISBN 9781644663646 (Paperback) | ISBN 9781623103620 (eBook)
Subjects: LCSH: Track and field athletes—Rating of—Juvenile literature. |
Track and field athletes—Records. | Olympic athletes—Juvenile literature. |
Olympics—History—Juvenile literature
Classification: LCC GV1060.55 .G57 2021 (print) | LCC GV1060.55 (ebook) |
DDC 796.42—dc23
LC record available at https://lccn.loc.gov/2019027609
LC ebook record available at https://lccn.loc.gov/2019027610

Printed in the United States. 2/20

All statistics are through the 2016 Olympic Games.

CONTENTS

Fast and

Sprinters are quick. Distance runners have long-lasting power. Track and field athletes are tough and strong. The best compete in the Summer Olympics.

The Summer Olympics are held every four years. Countries send their top athletes to the Games.

Powerful ATHLETES

Usain Bolt

Usain Bolt ruled sprinting. He never lost an Olympic final race. Bolt used his strong legs to power around the tracks.

Bolt was at his best in 2008. He set records in the 100-meter and 200-meter races.

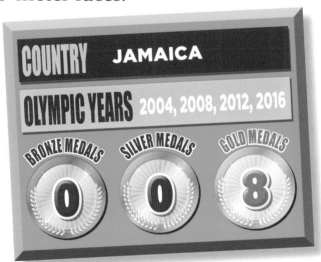

COUNTRY **JAMAICA**

OLYMPIC YEARS 2004, 2008, 2012, 2016

BRONZE MEDALS 0   SILVER MEDALS 0   GOLD MEDALS 8

In 2012 and 2016, Bolt won the same three events. He's the first runner to win three events in two straight Olympics.

TRACK AND FIELD EVENTS

The Games feature track and field events for men and women. Most events are held in a stadium.

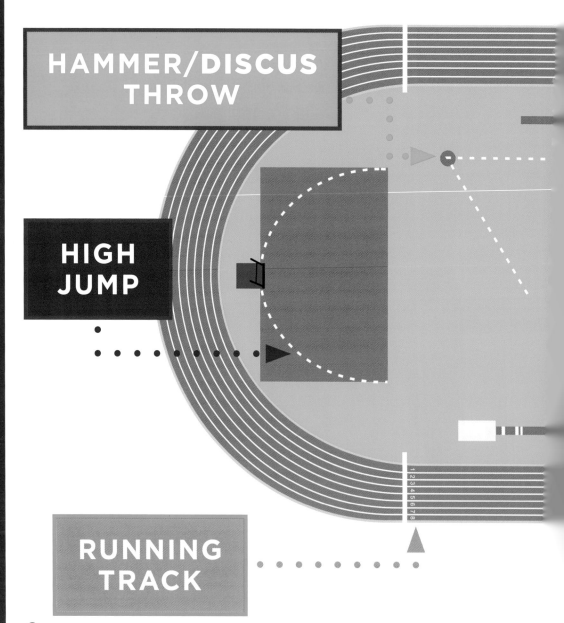

HAMMER/DISCUS THROW

HIGH JUMP

RUNNING TRACK

POLE VAULT

SHOT PUT

JAVELIN

LONG JUMP

9

Ray Ewry

Ray Ewry was an Olympic jumping superstar. He won every high jump and long jump he entered.

Ewry had **polio** as a child. He used jumping exercises to strengthen his legs. He became one of the strongest jumpers ever.

COUNTRY
UNITED STATES

BRONZE MEDALS
0

GOLD MEDALS
10

1900, 1904, 1906*, 1908
OLYMPIC YEARS

0
SILVER MEDALS

*In 1906, Greece held a special celebration. It was the 10th anniversary of the **modern** Olympic Games.

Top Olympic Track and Field Gold Medal Winners

10
RAY EWRY
(United States)

9
CARL LEWIS
(United States)

9
PAAVO NURMI
(Finland)

8
USAIN BOLT
(Jamaica)

6
ALLYSON FELIX
(United States)

Florence Griffith Joyner

Florence Griffith Joyner won a silver medal in 1984. But she was just getting started. She **dominated** four years later. The superstar earned three gold medals in 1988. She even set a world record in the 200-meter race.

COUNTRY	UNITED STATES	
OLYMPIC YEARS	1984, 1988	

BRONZE MEDALS	SILVER MEDALS	GOLD MEDALS
0	2	3

Jackie Joyner-Kersee

Jackie Joyner-Kersee was a powerhouse. She did the long jump and heptathlon. She scored more than 7,000 points in the heptathlon. She was the first to score that many. Her 7,291 points is still a world record.

COUNTRY	UNITED STATES
OLYMPIC YEARS	1984, 1988, 1992, 1996

BRONZE MEDALS	SILVER MEDALS	GOLD MEDALS
2	1	3

OLYMPIC HEPTATHLON

Women compete in the Olympic heptathlon.
It includes seven events.

- 800-METER RACE
- 100-METER HURDLES
- 200-METER RACE
- LONG JUMP
- SHOT PUT
- HIGH JUMP
- JAVELIN

Carl Lewis

Carl Lewis won gold medals at every Olympics he entered. Lewis set Olympic records in the 100-meter and 200-meter sprints. He also helped his **relay** teams set two Olympic records.

COUNTRY
UNITED STATES

BRONZE MEDALS
0

GOLD MEDALS
9

1984, 1988, 1992, 1996
OLYMPIC YEARS

1
SILVER MEDALS

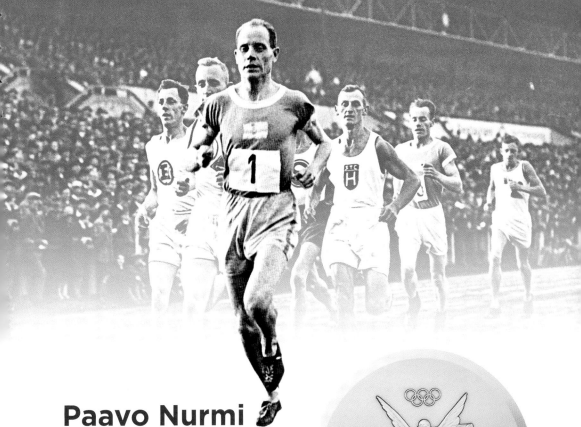

Paavo Nurmi

This long-distance runner was called the "Flying Finn." Paavo Nurmi had amazing long-distance speed. He set Olympic records in the 1,500-meter, 5,000-meter, and 10,000-meter runs.

COUNTRY **FINLAND**

OLYMPIC YEARS 1920, 1924, 1928

BRONZE MEDALS	SILVER MEDALS	GOLD MEDALS
0	3	9

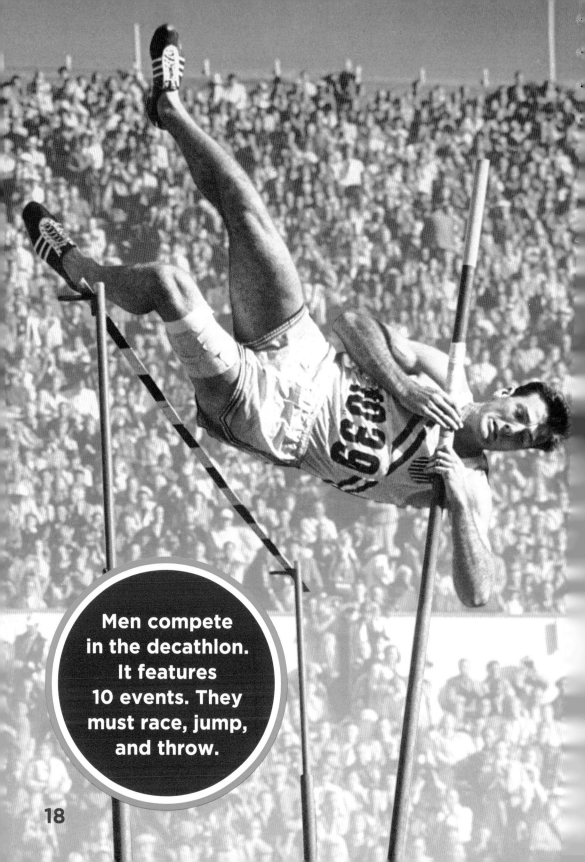

Men compete in the decathlon. It features 10 events. They must race, jump, and throw.

Bob Mathias

Bob Mathias was a decathlon athlete. He won it two times in a row. He was 17 years old at his first win. He set a world record in his second win.

COUNTRY	UNITED STATES	
OLYMPIC YEARS	1948, 1952	
BRONZE MEDALS	SILVER MEDALS	GOLD MEDALS
0	0	2

Al Oerter

Al Oerter had a powerful discus throw. He took gold in four Games in a row. And he set Olympic records in all of them!

COUNTRY
UNITED STATES

BRONZE MEDALS
0

GOLD MEDALS
4

1956, 1960, 1964, 1968
OLYMPIC YEARS

0
SILVER MEDALS

In 1968, Oerter threw for 212.5 feet (64.78 meters). That's longer than four school buses.

OLYMPIC RECORDS

HIGH JUMP

MEN'S RECORD	WOMEN'S RECORD
Charles Austin (United States)	Yelena Slesarenko (Russia)
7.841 FEET (2.39 M)	6.76 FEET (2.06 M)

MARATHON

MEN'S RECORD	WOMEN'S RECORD
Samuel Kamau Wanjiru (Kenya)	Tiki Gelana (Ethiopia)
2 HOURS, 6 MINUTES, 32 SECONDS	2 HOURS, 23 MINUTES, 7 SECONDS

100-METER RACE

MEN'S RECORD	WOMEN'S RECORD
Usain Bolt (Jamaica)	Florence Griffith Joyner (United States)
9.63 SECONDS	10.62 SECONDS

LONG JUMP

MEN'S RECORD

Bob Beamon
(United States)

29.199 FEET
(8.9 M)

WOMEN'S RECORD

Jackie Joyner-Kersee
(United States)

24.28 FEET
(7.4 M)

SHOT PUT

MEN'S RECORD

Ryan Crouser
(United States)

73.88 FEET
(22.52 M)

WOMEN'S RECORD

Ilona Slupianek
(East Germany*)

73.52 FEET
(22.41 M)

DISCUS THROW

MEN'S RECORD

Virgilijus Alekna
(Lithuania)

229.30 FEET
(69.89 M)

WOMEN'S RECORD

Martina Hellmann
(East Germany*)

237.2 FEET
(72.3 M)

*COUNTRY NO LONGER EXISTS

COUNTRY **UNITED STATES**

OLYMPIC YEARS **1936**

BRONZE MEDALS | SILVER MEDALS | GOLD MEDALS
0 | 0 | 4

Jesse Owens

Jesse Owens was an Olympic star in 1936. He won gold in four events. He set Olympic records in three of them.

Owens' wins were more than athletic wins. The 1936 Games were in Germany. The German leader was Adolf Hitler. Hitler believed black people weren't good enough to win. Owens proved him wrong.

Wilma Rudolph • • • • • • • • • • •

Wilma Rudolph was a great athlete. She had childhood polio. She couldn't walk without braces until age nine. But she became an Olympic star.

Rudolph ruled the sprints in 1960. She won the 100-meter and 200-meter races. She also helped her relay team earn gold.

**Rudolph set Olympic records in both
her sprint events in 1960.**

CHAPTER 3

Comparing

ATHLETES

Track and field athletes push to be
the best during the Summer Olympics.
Compare these Olympic greats.

TOTAL MEDALS

NUMBER OF MEDALS

	12	10	10	8	6
	Paavo Nurmi	Ray Ewry	Carl Lewis	Usain Bolt	Jackie Joyner-Kersee

OLYMPIC APPEARANCES

		NUMBER OF OLYMPIC APPEARANCES
Jesse Owens	1	
Florence Griffith Joyner	2	
Bob Mathias	2	
Wilma Rudolph	2	
Paavo Nurmi	3	
Usain Bolt	4	
Ray Ewry	4	
Jackie Joyner-Kersee	4	
Carl Lewis	4	
Al Oerter	4	

NUMBER OF OLYMPIC APPEARANCES

0　1　2　3　4

5

Florence Griffith Joyner

4

Al Oerter

Jesse Owens

Jesse Owens

4

Wilma Rudolph

2

Bob Mathias

discus (DIS-kus)—a heavy disk that is thrown for distance

dominate (DOM-uh-neyt)—to hold a commanding position over

javelin (JAV-lin)—a skinny metal pole thrown for distance

modern (MAH-durn)—relating to the period of time including the present and immediate past

polio (POH-lee-oh)—a disease that often affects children; it can cause muscle weakness or paralysis, often in the legs.

relay (REE-lay)—a race between teams in which each team member successively covers a portion of the course

shot put (SHAHT PUHT)—an event where a heavy metal ball is thrown for distance

sprinter (SPRINT-ur)—someone who runs at top speed for a short distance

BOOKS

Fretland VanVoorst, Jenny. *The Science Behind Track and Field.* STEM in the Summer Olympics. Minneapolis: Jump!, Inc., 2020.

Kortemeier, Todd. *12 Reasons to Love Track and Field.* Sports Report. Mankato, MN: 12 Story Library, 2018.

Osborne, M.K. *Track and Field.* Summer Olympic Sports. Mankato, MN: Amicus/Amicus Ink, 2020.

WEBSITES

Athletics – Summer Olympic Sport
www.olympic.org/athletics

Jackie Joyner-Kersee Biography: Olympic Athlete
www.ducksters.com/sports/jackie_joyner-kersee.php

Olympics Coverage from SI Kids
www.sikids.com/olympics

INDEX